Praise for *Total Succession*

"Having known Tyson for over 20 years, to this day, I have still not met a more innovative financial professional who is more client-centered and committed to adopting and deploying best practices. And there is no end in sight to Tyson's ongoing approach to leadership and pursuit of excellence."

–Duncan MacPherson
CEO, Pareto Systems
October 2025

"To witness Tyson Ray's evolution as a leader has been inspiring. His work began with the profound truth of *Total Relationship*, which created a positive ripple effect across the financial advisory community by reminding us that success is deeply human, not purely transactional. Now, with *Total Succession*, Tyson delivers the essential sequel, shifting the focus from individual connection to purposeful, organizational continuity. Creating a legacy firm that lasts beyond the founder is one of the most difficult challenges in business, but Tyson demystifies it. He provides a simple, systematic, and repeatable process for putting the right talent in the right seats and building a firm on purpose. This isn't just a book on transition; it's a masterclass in intentional organizational design for leaders who are ready to build something that truly outlasts them."

–Andrea Schlapia
Founder & CEO, Ironstone Business Coaching
November 2025

"I've always believed you should build your business like you're ready to sell it tomorrow. Not to leave, but to lead better. *Total Succession* captures that mindset perfectly. Tyson shows founders how to create lasting impact, protect their people, and leave a legacy that endures."

–Scott W. Danner
Executive Vice President, Head of Legacy at Steward Partners
October 2025

"Tyson and his team do a great job bringing open and transparent dialogue around difficult, yet critically important topics. His ability to balance the complicated world of succession planning through the lens of the advisor, the client, the acquirer, the banker, the psychologist, and the founder is exceptional."

–Dean Smith
Director of Business Development at Wealth Enhancement
October 2025

"In *Total Succession*, Tyson Ray delivers a by-an-advisor-for-advisors guide to one of the most important topics in our profession. Drawing on decades of real-world experience, he reminds us that succession isn't a single event—it's an ongoing process of reflection, preparation, and commitment. Tyson's perspective challenges every advisor to create the space to think intentionally about the future of their clients, teams, and families. This book is a must-read for any entrepreneur who wants to build an enduring enterprise that thrives beyond themselves."

–Nate Lenz
CEO, Concurrent
October 2025

"Tyson has created one of the most thoughtful and comprehensive succession guides I've ever read. Advisors face some very difficult realities as it relates to succession, and Tyson breaks those challenges down with logic, heart, and Midwest common sense. *Total Succession* is a must-read for every advisor, whether you have a succession plan in place or not."

–Peter Campagna
Managing Partner, Wise Rhino Group
November 2025

"Tyson Ray delivers a powerful reminder that great leadership isn't just about building. It's about believing in the people ready to rise next. *Total Succession* gives founders the mindset and roadmap to make that transition with grace, while giving permission to let go of what's no longer theirs to carry."

–Brittany Anderson
VP, Sweet Financial Partners
October 2025

"Preparation is everything. The advisors who plan their exits before they need to are the ones who win. *Total Succession* helps bring that to life. It's a guide for advisors who want to turn intention into action and build enterprise value that lasts."

–T. Ted Motheral, ESQ, MBA
Former Senior M&A Partner, The Potomac Law Group
October 2025

"One of the biggest gaps advisors and wealth managers have today, from my experience, is truly valued and trusted sources for accurate information about their businesses. Tyson Ray is one of those invaluable resources – whom you now have access to through this book! I've known Tyson for over a decade and count him among those on a very short list of people to turn to for all things best practice for wealth management. Those that have the opportunity to engage with him, and certainly the benefits his clients have received from working with him, are best of breed in the industry."

–**David Patchen**
Founder GBED Enterprises LLC
October 2025

"For any financial advisor, firm owner, or wealth manager who wants to build a lasting legacy, *Total Succession* is an essential read. This work goes far beyond the basic checklists and instead explores the nuanced challenges and human elements of transitioning a practice and FINISHING WELL. This book is a vital resource for anyone serious about the future of their firm, their legacy, and the well-being of their clients."

–**Brian Church**
Chief Growth Officer at OneAscent
Founder & CEO of Advisory DNA
October 2025

"Don't rush your transition. It took a long time to get to your level of success. Take the time needed to make sure it's ideal for you, your team, and clients. Get quality advice from those who have been through it. *Total Succession* helps founders do just that. It's the guide every founder needs to think about the exit they deserve, and how to do it with confidence and care."

–**Bryan Sweet**, CLU®, ChFC®, MSFS
Founder & Visionary, Sweet Financial Partners
October 2025

"In my work helping business owners and RIA principals plan and execute successful exits, I've learned that the best outcomes come from alignment — between values, vision, and structure. Across industries, the biggest missed opportunities we see are failing to properly prepare the business, define the details of your desired exit, and design what's next with purpose. *Total Succession* captures that balance perfectly, reframing succession as the beginning of a lasting legacy."

–**Nick Arellano, CFP®, CIMA®, CVA®, CEPA®**
Managing Partner, Your Legacy Partners
October 2025

Total Succession

5 Steps for Financial Advisors to Exit Confidently, Be Fully Compensated, and Keep Clients' Interests First

Other Books by Tyson Jon Ray

Total Relationship

Your World Impact: As A Financial Advisor

Total Succession

5 Steps for Financial Advisors to Exit
Confidently, Be Fully Compensated,
and Keep Clients' Interests First

Tyson Jon Ray

ethos
collective

Printed in the United States of America

Published by Igniting Souls
PO Box 43, Powell, OH 43065
IgnitingSouls.com

LCCN: 2025905099

Paperback ISBN: 978-1-63680-486-6
Hardback ISBN: 978-1-63680-487-3
eBook ISBN: 978-1-63680-488-0

Available in paperback, hardcover, e-book, and audiobook.

statements within this work. Responsibility for the views, depictions, and representations rests solely with the author.

The superscript symbol IP listed throughout this book is known as the unique certification mark created and owned by Instant IP[IP]. Its use signifies that the corresponding expression (words, phrases, chart, graph, etc.) has been protected by Instant IP[IP] via smart contract. Instant IP[IP] is designed with the patented smart contract solution (US Patent: 11,928,748), which creates an immutable time-stamped first layer and fast layer identifying the moment in time an idea is filed on the blockchain. This solution can be used in defending intellectual property protection. Infringing upon the respective intellectual property, i.e., IP, is subject to and punishable in a court of law.

Investment advisory services offered through FORM Wealth Advisors, LLC, an SEC-registered investment adviser. Registration does not imply a certain level of skill or training. For additional information, please review the firm's Form ADV at adviserinfo.sec.gov. This material is for educational purposes only and does not constitute investment advice or a recommendation to buy or sell any security. Reading this book does not create an adviser-client relationship.

CFP® | CERTIFIED FINANCIAL PLANNER™ Certified Financial Planner Board of Standards, Inc., owns the certification marks, which it awards to individuals who successfully complete initial and ongoing certification requirements.

CEPA® | The Exit Planning Institute (EPI) owns the certification mark CEPA®, a designation awarded to individuals who complete EPI's required education and credentialing requirements in exit planning.

CExP® | The Business Enterprise Institute(BEI) owns the certification mark CExP®, which it awards to individuals who successfully complete the organization's initial and ongoing educational and credentialing requirements focused on exit planning for business owners.

CIMA® | Investments & Wealth Institute™ (The Institute) is the owner of the certification marks "CIMA" and "Certified Investment Management Analyst." Use of CIMA and/or Certified Investment Management Analyst signifies that the user has successfully completed The Institute's initial and ongoing credentialing requirements for investment management professionals

DEDICATION

To the advisors who've built everything for
everyone else—
but never made space for themselves.
This is for you.

And to the team who gave me the space to create this—
your support made this possible.

CONTENTS

Part 2: Choose Your Own Adventure

INTRODUCTION

You *Will* Exit Your Practice.

Will You Lead It, or Will It Lead You?

Let's begin with something you already know: You *will* exit your practice.

You might not know when. You might not know how. But it will happen. One day, someone else will sit in your chair. Your phone will stop ringing. Your name will no longer be on the door.

The question is, will that moment reflect your values, or will it feel like something that happened to you, instead of something you led?

The truth is, most financial advisors are unprepared for succession. I've been in this industry for nearly three decades and sat across from advisors in every season of life—ambitious 30-somethings, overwhelmed 50-year-olds, and 70-year-olds who thought they had five more years until life said otherwise. I've coached, partnered, bought practices, and transitioned clients.

Across all those experiences, I've seen a pattern. The people who are best at helping others plan for the future often struggle to do it for themselves. Why? Because it's emotional. It's personal. And let's be honest, it's terrifying.

For most of us, this work is more than a job. It's identity, our purpose. This career gave us financial freedom and professional credibility, and it let us feel competent, needed, and respected. Whether you built your business from nothing or inherited it and kept it growing, you've poured every ounce of your energy into it and sacrificed your best years.

If you don't have the pieces in place for succession, let me offer some reassurance: You're not the only one who's overwhelmed. You're not behind. You're not broken. And it's not too late to do it well.

What matters most right now is that you're willing to face it.

The Leaky Pipes

There's a phrase I come back to often: *The plumber's pipes are leaking.*

Every field has experts who do brilliant work for everyone else but neglect things at home. In this case, it's you—the advisor who's helped hundreds of clients retire, sell businesses, and plan for the future without creating a clear path for your own.

You run review meetings as if they were second nature. You can craft financial plans in your sleep. Thousands have trusted you to transition wealth, navigate family dynamics, and deal with major life decisions. But when it comes to your own succession? It's uncomfortable and easy to put off.

You've probably said things like:

- "I've got some things in place."
- "I'm not quite ready yet."
- "I'll deal with that after the next hire, the next quarter, the next market shift…"

But let me tell you what I've learned the hard way: If you could have figured this out already, you would have.

Most of us don't delay succession planning because we're lazy or disorganized. We delay it because it's layered with emotional, relational, and financial complexity, and it's all wrapped up in ego, identity, and fear. No one teaches you how to untangle all that.

Until now.

Why I Wrote This Book

Several years ago, I thought I had my succession handled. I had a buy-sell agreement, a legal file with all the right signatures, and a written plan I thought made sense. But then I ran it through a real stress test, and I saw the cracks.

If something had happened to me—a car accident, an illness, even an unexpected opportunity—my team would've been unprepared. My clients wouldn't have known who to call, and the people I love most would have been left scrambling to piece together my intentions.

That's when I realized something painful: For all the planning I had done for others, I hadn't done it for myself—not fully, not well.

That moment changed me. It led me into the work of rebuilding, rethinking, and asking better questions—for myself, and for other advisors like you. I started talking to industry experts and walking alongside advisors who wrestled with their succession.

Some carried anxiety, self-doubt, and the fear of letting go or picking the wrong person. Others struggled between leaving money on the table and leaving a legacy behind.

I realized that when we don't lead our own transition, it hurts us, our team, our clients, and our families. Most importantly, it steals the confidence and peace we've helped so many others find.

That's why I wrote this book. Not to give you a rigid playbook, but to give you clarity. To provide a process that lets you own your exit with the same intentionality you've brought to your career.

Because you deserve that. The people who trust you deserve it, too.

Why This Matters Right Now

Let's talk numbers for a moment.

Of the more than 300,000 [1] financial advisors in the U.S., more than 100,000 [2] of them are expected to retire in the next ten years. Yet, fewer than 20 percent have a formal succession plan in place.[3]

At the same time, we're entering the greatest wealth transfer in modern history. Over 80 trillion dollars will move from one generation to the next in the next couple of decades[4], with firms like yours stewarding much of it.

This isn't some distant risk. This is *now*. And most firms are underprepared.

To make it worse, there's a talent gap. Fewer people are entering the industry, and many of those who do, don't want to take over or build a firm. They want structure, support, and work-life balance. That means the classic "sell it to the next-gen advisor" plan doesn't always work anymore.

If you don't understand your options, you won't see the difference until it's too late, and your clients will feel the ripple effects.

Which brings me to one more truth: this was never your money. It was always theirs.

You've spent a career earning trust. Don't jeopardize that now. Don't let your legacy end in confusion. You've worked too hard for too long to leave this open-ended.

Succession Is a Fiduciary Duty

You already understand the word fiduciary: to always put your client's best interest first. That responsibility doesn't stop just because you're ready to slow down. In fact, succession planning may be the final test of whether you've truly lived out your fiduciary duty.

Your clients trust you with their *future,* and when something changes—whether you step back gradually, sell the firm, or life intervenes unexpectedly—they deserve a plan. They deserve continuity. They deserve to know that their financial future won't be disrupted just because yours is.

Succession is about what's right for them, too.

I'm confident you've told a client to update their estate plan, create a will, or prepare their family for what comes next. This is the same thing. Your business should be just as prepared as your clients' estate documents. It's part of your responsibility, part of your promise.

If you want your clients to be taken care of after you're gone, it starts with taking care of this now. To exit well, you need a framework.

The Framework: SPACE

This book is built around a simple, powerful model I call **SPACE**:

See. Prepare. Act. Commit. Exit.

I love clever acronyms. But SPACE is more than that. It's a journey. Each stage is designed to help you uncover what matters, fix what's missing, make real decisions, and walk away with confidence.

- **See** is about defining your vision—for your life, your legacy, and your business
- **Prepare** is where you build a business that can stand on its own, even without you
- **Act** is where momentum begins, and loose ideas become real plans
- **Commit** is where you stop circling and step aside
- **Exit** is where you let go with clarity, compensation, and peace

You don't have to move through it overnight. You don't even have to do it perfectly. But you *do* have to start.

One Last Thought Before We Begin

You've done good work. You've changed lives. You've helped people retire with dignity and confidence.

Now it's your turn.

This book is about you. It's about the person behind the practice. It's about the relationships you've built and the impact you've made. This is your moment to make sure that the story doesn't end at the top of the mountain, but that it continues with intention, strength, and purpose.

You *will* exit your practice. I want to help make sure it reflects the best of what you've built.

Let's begin.

PART 1

The SPACE Framework[IP]— Your Guide to a Better Exit

CHAPTER 1

SEE THE LIFE YOU WANT BEYOND YOUR PRACTICE

Get Clarity on What Matters Most Before Planning Begins

Let me ask you something most advisors never slow down long enough to answer: What do you want life to look like when you're done running your practice?

This question isn't about how much you want to sell your business for or how many years you'll keep working part-time. I'm not asking whether you're planning for internal or external succession. I'm asking, what kind of life do you want to step into when this chapter closes?

Until you can see clearly beyond your practice, every tactic you chase will be a waste of time. You'll bounce between offers, team conversations, ideas about next-gen advisors, and well-meaning consultants, and nothing will stick because you're not aiming at anything real.

Before planning, structures, or strategy, we begin with vision.

The Vision We Skip

When most advisors first start thinking about succession, they go straight to the math:

- What's my business worth?
- How do I avoid getting crushed by taxes?
- Should I sell it to my team, or look for a buyer?

But none of those questions matter if you haven't done the deeper work.

Advisors are supposed to be planners, but when it comes to their own transitions, they skip the vision entirely. We're so used to solving other people's problems that we forget to look up and define what we're solving for ourselves.

I've asked many advisors this question: "What do you want your life to look like on the other side of the business?" Most commonly, I hear some version of "I haven't really thought about that yet." But this answer carries an inherent problem: You know what you're retiring from, but not what you're retiring into, and that's a recipe for regret.

The Henry Story

I worked with an advisor—we'll call him Henry—who built a successful practice over 40 years. He wanted to bring his sons into the business, but they resented it. They'd spent too many evenings waiting for their dad to come home from client meetings. By the time they graduated, they didn't want any part of it.

His daughter became his assistant, trying to keep the business in the family, but she never enjoyed the work. She ended up leaving to become a teacher after Henry finally retired.

And when he did retire, it was only because his wife passed away on their anniversary trip. He was 72. He waited too long.

Henry lacked vision, not options. He didn't take time to imagine life beyond the office. By the time he finally let go, some of the people he wanted to share it with were already gone. I don't want that to happen to you.

It's Okay Not to Know Yet

Here's something I want you to hear: It's okay if you don't know what's next. Often, you have been the one with all the answers, so sitting in the unknown may be new for you. It's also okay if you've spent decades pouring yourself into this business and now feel a little lost at the idea of not doing it anymore.

This business is consuming. It fills every corner. It gives us significance, affirmation, even identity. Sometimes it gives us more structure than our home life. This means the thought of stepping out of it feels more like stepping into a void than into a vision, but that's where the work begins.

You have to start asking yourself questions that go deeper than deal structure. Questions like:

- Who am I when I'm not the advisor anymore?
- What do I want to be remembered for?
- What do I want to give more of my time to: family, faith, health, mentoring, travel?
- What does a fulfilling week look like when I'm no longer the one solving everyone's financial problems?

Your personal vision and your professional vision have to work together because they've been intertwined for a long time. And that's why this first chapter is not about numbers. Instead, it's about your next narrative.

Cast a Clear Vision

Want to go deeper on crafting a vision for your exit? Listen to Episode 3 of the *Total Succession Podcast* where I break it down step-by-step.

You Deserve to Know What You're Aiming At

You don't have to figure it all out today, but you do need to start seeing something worth building toward.

It might be more time with your spouse or grandkids.

It might be coaching other advisors.

It might be getting your health back, or your soul back.

It might be finding new ways to serve, give, or create.

If you keep waiting to name it, your exit will start to feel like a loss instead of a launch. That's not what I want for you, and, deep down, I don't think that's what you want either.

Let's Pause Here

Before you read another chapter, I want you to pause and reflect. If you're like me, you're likely to skip this part, but you didn't pick up this book because you have your succession plan mapped out, so humor me and try this.

Take a breath. Let your mind go somewhere quiet. And then ask yourself:

- What do I want my life to look like after this business?
- What do I want to be present for that I've been missing?
- If I had a completely free week, how would I spend it?
- What am I afraid to admit I want?

Be honest. Write it down if it helps. You don't have to show it to anyone. Just start seeing it. Start naming it. That's where this begins.

You can't prepare for a future you haven't pictured. So, give yourself permission to imagine it. Get clear before you get tactical. SEE it, so you know what you're building toward.

Succession Planning Worksheet

Walk through the "See" and "Prepare" phases of the SPACE framework to define your vision and assess your readiness. Scan the code to view or download.

CHAPTER 2

PREPARE YOUR TEAM, CLIENTS, AND SYSTEMS

Build a Practice That's Transferable, Even if You're Not Selling It

Most advisors don't fail to transition their practice because they ran out of time. They fail because they waited too long to prepare. We tell ourselves we'll get to it when things slow down. But what happens if you don't get that chance? What happens if life interrupts your timeline?

Preparing your business is about protecting what you've already built. It's about making sure that if something happens to you—whether that's tomorrow or ten years from now—your clients, your team, and your family aren't left holding pieces of a plan that only existed in your head. You've seen this happen throughout your career with your clients, so you know firsthand what chaos can ensue from a lack of preparation.

This chapter is about readiness. Real succession planning starts when you stop assuming you'll always be the one showing up.

Let's talk about what that looks like.

What Makes a Business Transferable?

Let's get clear on this up front. A business is transferable when someone else can step in and run it without starting from scratch and with real continuity. A transferable business runs smoothly in relationships, expectations, processes, and communication—not just on paper.

This doesn't mean being ready to sell tomorrow. It doesn't even mean you plan to sell. Instead, it means you've built something that can survive your absence, and that matters because your absence is inevitable.

If you're the rainmaker, the head of ops, the client glue, and the marketing director, you don't have a sellable business. You have a job with your name on every description.

You can build your firm around you, or beyond you. One scales, sells, and survives. The other gets divided among the highest bidders.

Even if you're not thinking about selling, your *clients* are wondering what will happen after you're gone. As is your team. They want stability and clarity. If you can't give them those, the practice becomes a source of anxiety instead of assurance.

Gaps That Destroy Value and Create Chaos

When I reviewed my own internal succession plan, I had to face many things I didn't want to admit. We found gaps everywhere, and not just in the paperwork. There were gaps in the processes, people, and assumptions I'd been making for years.

Here are a few examples:

- Passwords. Only I knew them. Systems, tools—you name it. Locked for everyone but me.
- Cash flow. My team could move money, but did they understand why certain clients did things a certain way? Was it documented?
- Emergency plan. If something happened to me on a Thursday night, who would call the clients on Friday? Who would talk to compliance? Who will handle the check-in meeting I have scheduled for next week?

The gaps were real.

Here's what hit me hard: even if the business didn't collapse, it would stall. Clients would feel it. Morale would dip. My family would be stuck piecing together instructions from sticky notes and folders. I didn't want that, and you don't want it either.

Prepare Like You're Going to Sell, Even If You're Not

Scott Danner said it best: "You should always be ready to sell your business." Why? Because the process of preparing to sell makes your practice stronger, even if you never sell it. When you get serious about making your practice transferable, you start fixing the stuff that you've been tolerating for too long.

- You clean up the tech stack, stop doing five jobs, and start hiring for key roles.
- You tighten your client onboarding.
- You build a real bench that goes beyond support staff.
- And most importantly, you stop being the single point of failure.

I know that sounds intense, but let me ask you this: what happens if your best client calls tomorrow and you're unavailable? What does that experience feel like for them? Are they reassured? Or do they quietly wonder if it's time to look elsewhere?

If you answer, "My assistant would take a message," you've got work to do.

Always Be Ready to Sell
Scott Danner shares how sale-ready gave him more freedom. Hear his story and what it really means to let go without leaving.

Prepare the People, Not Just the Systems

When advisors think about succession readiness, they often focus on systems: the processes, workflows, and compliance documents that keep the business running. But systems alone can't lead your business.

If you want the option of an internal succession down the road, you need to prepare leaders now. Not just support staff or service reps, but real next generation (G2) talent—people who can think strategically, carry relationships, manage complexity, and eventually take the reins. Those people don't just show up ready. You have to build the bench.

Internal succession, whether your successor is a next-gen advisor, a family member, or an in-house leader, relies on you investing years in developing their skills, confidence, and leadership voice. You didn't build this practice in a year, so you can't expect them to take it over in a year.

Succession is earned, not given.

How to Build Your Bench (Before You Need It)

At my firm, FORM Wealth Advisors, we created a path for the next generation of advisors. Here's what that looks like:

- **Internship Program:** We designed a hands-on internship that gives young talent exposure to real work, real clients, and real mentorship. This helps us identify people with both the technical chops and the emotional intelligence to grow with us.
- **Mentorship & Shadowing:** We created opportunities for next-gen advisors to sit in on client reviews, run pre-meeting prep, and gradually own parts of the relationship before they are ever "in charge."

- **Career Ladders**: We created growth tiers that let every advisor know what is expected at each level. That clarity motivates growth and creates accountability. Next-gen advisors can see the path, not just guess.
- **Succession Conversations Early:** We don't wait until someone is "ready" to talk about leadership. We plant the idea early and let their ambition grow into it.

You don't need a dozen candidates. You need one or two people with real potential and a clear path.

If your firm only works because *you* are the brain, the heart, and the name on the door, then it's not succession-ready. The best succession planning starts before you need it, not with contracts or valuations, but with leadership development. The more you invest in your people, the more options you'll have when it's time to step away. Prepare the systems, yes. But prepare the successors, too.

How to Build Your Bench

Learn how to build next-gen talent from the ground up in this episode: A 5-Stage Path to Building Advisor Talent from Within.

POPULAR

Begin with the Truth

Here's how you begin. Make a list of every function in your business:

- Marketing
- Client service
- Compliance
- Strategic planning
- Recruiting
- Leadership
- File organization
- Tech
- Other

Now, put your name next to every one of those things that currently depend on you. Be brutally honest. If you're the backup, that counts too.

Now look at that list. That's your job. That's what someone else would have to do if you were gone. If it makes you nervous, good. Take it as your sign to start transitioning responsibilities. You don't need to solve everything today, but you do need to acknowledge what would break and start fixing it.

From Advisor to Architect

Once you see the gaps, the next step is shifting your mindset.

You're no longer just the advisor. You are the architect of a practice that can operate without you. That means:

- You document what you know so others can use it.
- You train your team to lead, not just to assist.
- You stop hoarding client relationships and start sharing them.
- You build systems that deliver consistency, not just excellence that depends on your mood.

For everything you don't like doing, there's someone else who loves it. Just because you're great at something doesn't mean you should still be the one doing it. The more you shift into the role of architect, the more margin you create for what really matters: your vision, your people, and your eventual exit.

You Might Need More Than One You

Here's something a lot of founders don't realize until they're in the middle of a deal: It might take more than one person to replace you. You've worn every hat for years: CEO, lead advisor, head of growth, mentor, rainmaker, spreadsheet whisperer. You did it because you had to. That's how most of us built our businesses.

But if you plan to step back or transition out, you can't assume one next-gen advisor will step in and do it all. They might need a partner, an operations manager, time, coaching, or a support structure that didn't exist when you started. That doesn't mean your successor is weak. It means the business has outgrown the founder model. That's a good thing.

Plan accordingly.

Start Now, Even If You're Not Ready

You can take the first step today: pick one thing only you know how to do and teach someone else how to do it. Write the instructions; record a video; create a checklist; bring your team into the room as you walk through it so they can ask you questions. Just do one thing.

Every time you prepare, you create capacity— capacity for others to grow, for you to let go, and for your business to thrive without you. You don't have to sell your practice, but you should build it as if you would. That's how you protect what you've built and honor the people who helped you grow. That's how you prepare to exit well.

Succession Planning Worksheet

Walk through the "See" and "Prepare" phases of the SPACE framework to define your vision and assess your readiness. Scan the code to view or download.

CHAPTER 3

ACT WHILE YOU HAVE TIME

Turn Intention Into Action,
One Decision at a Time

Every advisor I know has good intentions. We want to do the right thing. We want to protect our clients, honor our team, provide for our families, and leave a practice we're proud of. But intentions without action are just unexecuted ideas.

In this chapter, I want to help you move from thinking about succession to actually doing something about it. This isn't about making a giant leap or a dramatic exit. It's just about movement and momentum, because once you start moving, clarity follows.

One of the biggest mistakes I see advisors make is waiting for certainty. We tell ourselves we'll act when we know exactly what we want, who the successor should be, or what the market says our business is worth. You don't ask clients to time the

49

market or wait for perfect conditions. Why expect that of yourself when it comes to planning your own future?

Clarity doesn't come before action. It comes because of it.

The Power of a First Step

I remember working with an advisor who kept saying he wanted to exit "in the next few years." But when I asked what steps he had taken, his answer was always the same: "We're still talking about it." That conversation went on for three years.

Eventually, we sat down and made a list of things he could do that month. Not massive changes, just simple steps to create forward motion:

1. Assigning a team lead.
2. Documenting his client review process.
3. Meeting with a valuation expert.
4. Writing a vision letter to his family.

It didn't take long for one step to turn into two and two into four. Within a year, he had not only defined his exit plan, but he had also restructured his team, created career paths, and started mentoring his potential successor—all because he finally moved.

The hardest part is getting out of neutral.

Action Reveals Reality

You might have a story in your head about how your team will react to succession conversations. Your story might include how your clients will feel about your leaving or what a potential buyer might say about your business. But until you take action, you don't actually know.

You might be surprised how much your team appreciates the honesty, how much your clients respect the plan, or the relief your spouse feels when you finally put something in writing.

More than once, I've seen advisors stall for years, only to discover that the resistance they feared wasn't real. It was a story they told themselves. The act of moving revealed a different reality, one far more hopeful than they expected.

You Won't Know Until You Move

Hear Duncan MacPherson talk about how most of the resistance you're worried about lives in your head. Once you take action, the real story unfolds.

Small Decisions, Big Impact

You don't need to take giant leaps to make progress. In fact, big leaps are rare. Most real succession plans are built decision by decision—one conversation, one policy update, one delegated responsibility, one documented process.

Here are a few examples of high-impact, low-resistance actions:

- Record a short video or voice memo explaining "why I built this firm."
- Decide what you're no longer going to say yes to.
- Set a "Decision Date" for something you've been delaying and share that date with someone who will hold you accountable.

None of those actions requires perfection, but all of them move the plan forward.

Remember: succession isn't a single decision. It's a series of decisive steps. If you wait to feel ready, you'll wait forever. The truth is, no one ever feels fully ready to exit their life's work. But you don't have to start with the end. You just have to start. The longer you wait, the heavier it gets, so let's get moving.

CHAPTER 4

COMMIT TO LETTING GO
SO OTHERS CAN STEP IN

What You Release Now
Makes Room for What's Next

There comes a point in every advisor's journey where strategy, planning, and prep work are no longer the issue. You've initiated conversations and outlined a path forward. You've taken some action, but something still holds you back.

That something is *you*.

No matter how well-crafted your plan, the moment will arrive where you have to decide: Am I ready to step aside so someone else can step in?

This is where succession moves from intellectual to emotional, from external to internal, from theoretical to personal. This chapter is about that shift.

Why Letting Go Is So Hard

Letting go of your business is one of the most emotional moves you'll ever make. Releasing control, identity, and rhythm is never easy.

For years, maybe most of your life, this work has been your calling card. It's where you've made your impact, built your reputation, and found your confidence. If you're honest, it's probably where you still feel most useful. So, of course, it's hard to let go.

But the longer you wait to commit, the more you slow down everything that comes next. Your team stays stuck in limbo. Your clients stay uncertain. Your successor stays on the sidelines. Your family stays guessing. There is no momentum without commitment.

How to Know If You're Still Acting or Finally Committing

ACT and COMMIT can look similar from the outside. But the difference is everything.

You're likely still ACTING if:

- You're still running point on all key relationships.
- You've started succession tasks but haven't given away authority.
- You feel energized by the plan but uncomfortable releasing control.

You'll know you're COMMITTING when:

- You've told your successor, team, or family what role you will *no longer* play.
- You've started stepping out of client-facing leadership.
- You're preparing emotionally to be out of the center.

The shift happens when your actions move from preparation to permission. When you start letting others step in as you step back from the spotlight, you'll know you've begun to commit. It happens when you no longer need to be involved in every decision.

What Commitment Sounds Like

When you truly commit, your language changes. Your conversations move from:

I still want to be involved in everything.	→	I want others to own more than they ever have.
Let me handle this one.	→	You've got this. I trust you.
They're not quite ready.	→	They'll grow by doing this.
This is my legacy.	→	I want the firm to reflect our values.

Commitment releases with intention. You don't vanish. You choose where to invest your influence. You stop showing up everywhere and start showing up where it matters most, where only you can.

You can plan forever, but if you never commit, your succession won't happen. Not the way it needs to. The real work now is about letting go of what you don't need to carry anymore. What you release now makes room for what's next, and that's when the transition becomes real.

CHAPTER 5

EXIT WITH CONFIDENCE AND PURPOSE

It's Not an End; It's Your New Beginning

We talk about exits like they're clean breaks or finish lines. But for most advisors, their exit is never as simple as a handshake, a deal, a speech, or a sunset. If you've poured decades into your practice, you won't walk away in a single moment. It will take a series of moments. Most advisors need a slow release or shift in posture.

What comes next matters just as much as what came before.

Exit = Transformation

Too many advisors treat their exit like a business deal. Yes, it involves financial, legal, and operational elements. But your exit is way more than that.

You're not just transferring equity. You're releasing identity.

You're not just walking away. You're walking toward something new.

To do that well, you need to think like a founder and allow yourself to feel like a human. Give yourself permission to be honest about what transitioning means emotionally, relationally, and even spiritually.

I know. It's hard. For decades, you've been "the one."

The one everyone turned to.

The one who had the answers.

The one who was responsible.

Suddenly, your role shifts. If you haven't done the emotional work, that shift can feel like loss. You're leaving behind an identity, your morning rhythm, your decision-making power, your sense of usefulness, your calendar, your inbox, and your name on the door.

Depending on how deeply tied your self-worth is to your work, this can feel like a kind of death. That's why so many advisors delay the exit, try to sneak out quietly, or worse—retire without ever really letting go.

But what if your exit could also feel like relief? Like freedom? Like renewal?

The key is acknowledging the grief so you can embrace the gain. The best way to do that is to start defining what you're moving toward *before* you finish stepping away.

Bryan Sweet of Sweet Financial Partners once shared how difficult it was to imagine life after the firm, until he began mentoring other advisors. That became his new calling, his next mission. He didn't fade out. He evolved.

Transformation is the ideal model. You don't vanish; you surface reimagined. You recognize you aren't quitting; you're redirecting your purpose.

Make the Ending Clear

One of the worst things you can do is exit quietly. Fizzling out and disappearing behind the scenes isn't good for you or those your exit impacts. Your clients, team, and family deserve clarity. They deserve a *moment*, something they can look back on and say: "That's how it happened. And it happened well."

You deserve that moment, too.

Say it out loud. Name what you're stepping into. Share your gratitude. Celebrate what you've built and who helped you build it. Don't downplay it. Honor it.

The people in your life who watched you sacrifice to build this practice deserve to share in the celebration. They've made sacrifices alongside you.

If honoring your own hard work feels uncomfortable, think of it instead as acknowledging theirs. It could look like:

- A formal announcement to clients.
- A private dinner with your leadership team.
- A public message or letter expressing thanks and vision.
- A conversation with your spouse about what this means for your relationship and rhythm.
- An intentional last client meeting, where you express your trust in the team.
- A walk through the office to shake hands and share stories.

You don't need a retirement party (though you might enjoy it), but you do need something that signifies intentional closure. A clean ending creates space for a meaningful beginning.

Leave as Well as You Led

You spent your career guiding others through transition. Now it's your turn. You're not just an advisor anymore. You're an example. The way you exit will teach others how to exit. Your team is watching. Your clients are watching. Your family is watching. The next generation is watching.

Let them see what it looks like to step away with integrity, joy, and purpose—not because you have to, but because you're ready.

You've Seen the life you want beyond your exit

You've Prepared your team and done the work.

You've Acted; taken the steps, and transferred the trust.

You've Committed to letting go.

Now it's time to Exit.

But this isn't the end. It's your next beginning, and it's worth showing up for.

PART 2

Choose Your Own Adventure

CHAPTER 6

YOUR OPTIONS, EXPLAINED INTERNAL VS. EXTERNAL SUCCESSION

Know the Tradeoffs and Choose with Confidence

Most advisors assume they'll transition their business to someone they already know: a next-gen advisor, a longtime employee, or a family member. That's the industry default. It feels safe, loyal, and familiar. But that's not your only option. There may be a path that better fits your values, team, clients, and vision for life after the firm. That's what this section is about.

Even though you're reading this after the EXIT chapter, this decision point actually belongs much earlier in the process, often during the SEE or PREPARE stage. The path you choose will shape everything else: how you train your team, what kind of systems you need, how you communicate with clients, even how you define your timeline.

This chapter will give you a high-level view of your two main succession options:

- **Internal Succession:** transitioning the firm to someone within.
- **External Succession:** selling or merging with someone outside.

In the chapters that follow, I'll outline what each one means, why it matters, and the broad pros and cons of both. I'll also break down the sub-paths inside each option. But first, let's get clear on the landscape.

What Is Internal Succession?

Internal succession means transitioning your business to someone already within your firm: a next-gen advisor, a business partner, a G2 leader, or a rising team member who's earned your trust. This is often seen as the most relational path. People like the continuity, loyalty, and legacy this path offers. You know them. They know your clients. The handoff feels more like mentoring than selling.

High-Level Pros of Internal Succession	High-Level Cons of Internal Succession
Greater relational continuity with clients	Often slower and more complex
Stronger cultural alignment	Successor may lack capital or readiness
More control over the timeline and structure	Can strain existing team dynamics
Opportunity to mentor your successor directly	If not structured carefully, it can drag out and hurt value
Seen by many clients and teams as the most "loyal" choice	

The internal path is often more emotionally driven. It feels personal, but that doesn't mean it's always the best fit, especially if the internal bench isn't deep or ready.

A Story from the Other Side

Most books on succession planning are written from the founder's point of view. And that's fair, it's your firm, decision, and legacy on the line.

But before I ever thought about selling my own practice, I was on the other side of the table. I was the next-gen advisor. No one handed me a five-year development plan. I was just the kid who was hungry to learn. I worked hard and watched how clients were treated. I paid attention to what mattered. Over time, I earned more responsibility, and eventually, when the founder was ready to step back, I stepped in because we had built something worth continuing.

Internal succession is personal for me. It shaped my career. It gave me a calling. It showed me firsthand what's possible when a founder is willing to bet on someone younger, hungrier, and still figuring it out, but committed.

Now, decades later, I'm on the other side of the table. I'm the founder, and I've had to ask myself: *Am I willing to do for others what someone once did for me?*

That's the real test of internal succession. It requires humility, patience, and courage, as well as a willingness to believe in someone else's future as much as you once believed in your own. That belief changed my life, and it might be what changes your firm's future. So, when I talk about internal succession—not just as an option, but as a calling—I'm remembering, not guessing. It worked for me because someone believed in building something that would last beyond them. Can you, too?

What Is External Succession?

External succession means selling or transitioning your firm to a third party, another advisor or peer, a national aggregator or integrator, a buyer backed by private equity, or a combination of options.

This path is often more transactional. It can also be cleaner, faster, and more financially compelling, especially if the internal path isn't viable.

High-Level Pros of External Succession	High-Level Cons of External Succession
Often faster	Potential cultural disconnect
Brings in outside expertise, systems, and support	Greater risk of client or team attrition
May result in higher valuation	Less personal influence over future firm direction
Can protect the business when no internal option exists	May feel like a "sale" instead of a "legacy"

There's nothing wrong with going external. In fact, for many advisors, it's the most logical and protective path. However, you have to be honest about what matters most to you: control, continuity, compensation, or culture.

The Truth: There's No Perfect Path

Every advisor brings different goals, team dynamics, and client expectations into this decision. That's why I created the SPACE framework first: without doing that inner work, this outer decision is often rushed, emotional, or based on fear.

There is no one-size-fits-all solution, just the fit that aligns with your values and your vision.

In the next chapters, I'll break down the pros, cons, structures, and emotional realities of each sub-path:

- Internal succession to a next-gen advisor or team
- Selling or joining a team within your same broker-dealer
- M&A with a peer or partner
- External sale to an aggregator or integrator
- Strategic partnership with a PE-backed source
- Combination of sub-paths

But for now, I want you to sit with this question someone once asked me: If you weren't afraid of letting someone down, which path would feel most aligned?

CHAPTER 7

INTERNAL SUCCESSION

Sell to a Team or Family Member, or Sell or Join a Team with the Same Custodian

Internal succession is the path most advisors assume they'll take, but few fully understand what it demands. It often feels most natural to hand off the business to someone you've trained, mentored, and worked beside. Handing the reins to someone who shares your values, understands your clients, and has already bought into the culture you've built feels most comfortable.

But there are multiple ways internal succession can unfold, and each version has unique advantages, risks, and best practices.

Option 1: Sell to a Team Member or G2 Leader

Selling to a team member or next-gen leader is the traditional approach. It happens when an advisor sells equity or full ownership to one or more next-gen team members who are already embedded in the firm.

Pros of Selling to a Team Member or G2 Leader	Cons of Selling to a Team Member or G2 Leader
Strong relational continuity with clients	Successor may not have access to financing
Cultural alignment is already in place	Valuation may need to be discounted or seller-financed
Allows for a gradual handoff and mentorship	Risk of entitlement if successor hasn't earned ownership
Preserves the internal team structure and morale	Deal structures can drag out over years, causing uncertainty

There are a few best practices to keep in mind when transitioning to a next-gen advisor:

1. **Start Succession Conversations 5–10 Years Out**

   - Begin with informal discussions about future vision, ownership goals, and readiness.
   - Use tools like leadership assessments or behavioral profiles to evaluate true leadership capacity.
   - Avoid "tap on the shoulder" succession with no structure or accountability.

2. **Use Independent Valuation (and Refresh it Periodically)**

   - Bring in a third-party firm for a professional valuation to remove emotional bias.
   - Reassess every 2–3 years to reflect firm growth, market conditions, or role changes.
   - Share valuation rationale with successors to promote transparency and buy-in.

3. **Design a Multi-Phase Deal with Clear Benchmarks**

   - Tie ownership tranches to measurable outcomes (e.g., client retention, business development, leadership participation).
   - Use performance-based vesting.

- Consider equity "earn-ins" alongside buy-ins to reinforce accountability.

4. **Explore Flexible Financing Options**

   - Don't assume seller-financing is the only path; research SBA loans, partner banks, internal financing via retained earnings, or shared risk structures.
   - Evaluate using an ESOP, profit-sharing, or phantom equity as stepping stones to ownership.
   - Introduce potential successors to trusted lenders early to assess viability.

5. **Build a Real Development Plan**

   - Map out a leadership development track with specific training, mentorship, and accountability.
   - Give G2s strategic responsibilities early: sit in on owner-level decisions, lead initiatives, manage profit centers.
   - Define the difference between "being an advisor" and "being an owner."

6. **Codify Roles, Expectations & Legal Agreements**

   - Draft operating agreements that define voting rights, roles, dispute resolution, and ownership transfer triggers.

- Establish a clear operating framework for post-transition governance.
- Review and update buy-sell agreements regularly as conditions change.

7. Create and Execute a Formal Client Transition Plan

- Segment top clients and assign a co-lead structure with the successor at least 12–24 months before final transition.
- Communicate clearly and consistently with clients to build confidence in the G2's capabilities.
- Measure and track client retention and satisfaction throughout the handoff process.

8. Align Internal Culture Around the Transition

- Hand off *and* communicate leadership; clarify to staff who's taking the lead and why.
- Celebrate early wins publicly; let the team feel momentum.
- Hold team Q&A sessions to build alignment and confidence in the new leadership.

Option 2: Sell to a Family Member

Some founders choose a son, daughter, or relative to take over the practice. This can be meaningful and deeply personal, but it can also blur the line between family and business.

Pros of Selling to a Family Member	Cons of Selling to a Family Member
Preserves family legacy and founder's name	Can create internal team resentment or perceived favoritism
Shared long-term values and vision	May lead to misalignment if the successor isn't fully committed
Strong motivation to protect the business and clients	Risk of family conflict bleeding into business decisions

There are a few best practices to keep in mind when transitioning to a family member:

1. **Treat the Successor as an Employee First, Family Second**

   - Require the next-gen family member to earn credibility inside and outside the firm.
   - Have them work in another firm or industry before joining yours (3–5 years recommended).

- Place them in non-leadership roles first to build technical competence, humility, and perspective.

2. **Require a Structured Career Path with Milestones**

- Outline specific skill and leadership benchmarks before equity is considered.
- Tie ownership or partnership to performance metrics: production, client service, management, etc.
- Make promotions contingent on achieving predefined milestones vs. family status.

3. **Clarify Roles to Avoid Power Struggles**

- Use written job descriptions and org charts to define each person's lane, even if they share a last name.
- Avoid co-leadership ambiguity (e.g., "Mom still runs everything but also wants her son to lead").
- If multiple family members are involved, establish clear reporting lines and decision-making authority.

4. **Leverage Third-Party Consultants and Coaches**

- Bring in succession advisors or family business consultants to mediate sensitive conversations.

- Use an outside board or advisory council to give objective feedback and guidance.
- Create space for honest dialogue about expectations, readiness, and vision.

5. **Address Team Dynamics Head-On**

- Proactively communicate the "why" behind the family member's role to the broader team.
- Hold regular all-staff meetings to keep culture, alignment, and morale intact.
- Consider anonymous staff surveys or check-ins to uncover hidden friction or favoritism concerns.

6. **Plan for "What If They Leave?"**

- Draft a contingency plan if the family member changes direction or leaves the business.
- Have a formal employment and equity agreement that includes exit terms, buyback clauses, and valuation methodology.
- Avoid giving away large ownership stakes before they've demonstrated long-term commitment.

7. Avoid Skipping Steps Just Because They're Family

- Don't fast-track them into leadership roles without full seasoning, especially in client-facing, operational, or compliance areas.
- Ensure they spend time learning every aspect of the business, including client service, operations, compliance, and growth strategy.
- Consider a "shadow period" where they co-lead with the founder before stepping fully into the seat.

8. Align Family Vision with Business Vision

- Have dedicated off-site sessions to explore long-term family and business alignment.
- Discuss values, legacy, client continuity, and expectations openly.
- Write a "family mission statement" or succession charter to codify what matters most.

Option 3: Join or Sell to Another Team on the Same Platform

Another form of internal succession involves combining forces with another advisor or team that shares your custodian, broker-dealer, or platform.

This allows for more scale and structure, while maintaining some continuity.

Pros of Selling to Another Team on the Same Platform	Cons of Selling to Another Team on the Same Platform
Easier integration due to shared systems and custodians	May require culture blending and client communication
Potential for higher valuation through increased scale	Less personal connection than with your own internal team
Successor already understands the operating environment	Could create turf tension if roles aren't clearly defined
Allows you to reduce ownership while staying semi-active	

There are a few best practices to keep in mind when transitioning to another team on the same platform:

1. **Align Philosophically *Before* You Talk Structure**

   - Start by aligning values and client philosophy.
   - Ask: How do they define client success? How do they communicate? What's their service model?

- If client, team, or cultural alignment is off—it's a nonstarter, no matter how "compatible" the tech stack looks.

2. **Build a Clear Roadmap for Ownership & Leadership**

   - Document the transition timeline, roles during and after the handoff, and how decisions will be made.
   - Outline voting rights, profit-sharing, and operational responsibilities clearly— especially if you plan to stay involved for a while.
   - Include off-ramps or unwind clauses if either party wants out mid-integration.

3. **Design a Thoughtful, Phased Client Transition Plan**

   - Build co-branded messaging around the *why* of the merger: enhanced service, better continuity, aligned values.
   - Assign client segments to primary and secondary relationship managers in advance.
   - Use warm handoffs via joint meetings, custom letters, and targeted outreach.

4. **Protect Culture with Structured Integration Steps**

- Host joint team events, roundtables, and informal interactions before announcing any formal merger.
- Share playbooks and SOPs to identify overlaps, gaps, and differences early.
- Assign an internal integration lead or committee to oversee communication, conflict resolution, and team morale.

5. **Lock in Legal, Compliance & HR Early**

- Consult platform relationship managers or transition specialists for guidance specific to your custodian or BD.
- Address titles, licensing, supervisory roles, and revenue splits ahead of time.
- Anticipate complications if either team has legacy platform agreements or trailing liabilities.

6. **Plan for Platform Nuances**

- Even within the same BD or custodian, team structures, payout grids, compliance cultures, and CRM usage can differ.
- Test systems compatibility (tech, billing, client reporting) in a sandbox environment before going live.

- Get platform pre-approval if necessary for formal mergers, repapering strategies, or OSJ changes.

7. **Communicate Transparently with Staff and Stakeholders**

- Don't let rumors spread; explain the "why" to your team early and bring them into the transition plan.
- Set expectations around career paths, compensation changes, and reporting lines.
- Involve key staff from both sides in planning, so they become champions—not blockers—of the new structure.

8. **Focus on the Long-Term Win, Not Short-Term Control**

- Successful integrations are built on mutual benefit.
- Be open to hybrid roles, shared decision-making, and evolving responsibilities.
- Know when to lead, when to follow, and when to let go.

When Familiar Isn't Always Simple

The people closest to us often feel like the safest succession option, but familiarity doesn't eliminate complexity; it often adds layers to it. Advisors pursuing internal transitions sometimes discover that the emotional ties, unspoken expectations, and blurred boundaries make this path harder to lead with objectivity. That doesn't mean it's the wrong choice, but it does mean you have to be ruthlessly honest about readiness: yours and theirs.

Internal Succession Comparison

Succession Option	Best Fit For	Pros	Cons
Sell to a Team Member	Advisors with tenured staff showing leadership	• Strong client continuity • Cultural alignment • Preserves internal morale	• May lack financing • Entitlement risk • Long deal timelines
Sell to a Family Member	Advisors with relatives in or entering the business	• Preserves Legacy • Shared values • High personal meaning	• Can create resentment • Family conflict risk • May lack commitment
Sell to a Team with same Custodian or BD	Advisors looking for scale while maintaining partial control	• Shared systems • Cultural familiarity • Partial liquidity	• Role confusion • Turf tension • Requires strong leadership alignment

As you consider what's next, keep your options open. The best path forward may not be the one you've assumed from the beginning. It might be outside your current team, your network, or even your comfort zone. In the next chapter, we will explore external succession, what it really looks like, who it's right for, and why more advisors are choosing it as their most aligned exit strategy.

CHAPTER 8

EXTERNAL SUCCESSION

Sell to Another Advisor, an Aggregator or Integrator, a Private Equity Company, or a Combination of Options

External succession used to be a dirty word in the wealth management industry. It meant you were selling out—giving up and letting go of your legacy. That stigma is fading fast and for good reason. Today, external succession isn't a backup plan. For many advisors, it's the smartest, cleanest, and most strategic way to protect what they've built and create the future they actually want.

If your internal bench isn't deep, if the timing doesn't work, or if your successor lacks the capital or experience to take the reins, then it may be time to look beyond your walls.

Let's look at your external options.

Option 1: Sell to Another Advisor or Local Peer

This approach involves transitioning your practice to an outside advisor who is a peer, often in your same region or network. Sometimes this happens organically through local groups, masterminds, or years of industry connection.

Pros of Selling to Another Advisor or Peer	Cons of Selling to Another Advisor or Peer
Shared understanding of the business model and client needs	Can be difficult to vet readiness or long-term commitment
Potential for cultural fit if values align	May lead to personality or leadership clashes
Deal terms can be more flexible	Integration of teams and processes can be messy without structure
Can create a win-win for both clients and successor	

There are a few best practices to keep in mind when transitioning to another advisor or peer:

1. **Build the Relationship Before You Build the Deal**

   - Spend time in real conversations.
   - Look for evidence of how they treat clients, staff, and partners over time; shared geography or years in the same study group isn't enough.
   - Observe how they handle pressure, lead people, and solve client issues before inviting them into your legacy.

2. **Align on Vision and Client Philosophy from Day 1**

   - Use case studies or client scenarios to see how they'd handle common financial planning decisions, communication styles, and risk tolerance issues.
   - Discuss client segmentation, service models, and what makes an ideal client; misalignment here will break trust later.
   - Talk through "non-negotiables" like fiduciary standards, fee structures, or service expectations.

3. **Don't DIY the Deal Structure—Bring in Third-Party Support**

   - Use an M&A consultant or succession planning specialist to help with valuation, terms, earnouts, clawbacks, and contingencies.

- Leverage legal and tax professionals who specialize in advisory practice transitions.
- Create a clear Letter of Intent and Purchase Agreement with all assumptions spelled out.

4. **Map Out a Detailed Post-Sale Integration Plan**

- Who is the face of the firm during the transition period?
- When and how are client relationships transferred, and in what order?
- What happens to your staff: are they retained, retrained, or reassigned?
- Include a 6–12-month roadmap with checkpoints for client retention, culture alignment, and team communication

5. **Establish Clear Roles for You (the Seller) After the Sale**

- Define whether you'll stay on in an advisory, mentorship, or emeritus capacity—and for how long.
- Document how and when you'll communicate with clients, attend meetings, or introduce the successor.
- Avoid the "two captains" scenario—be visible, but not confusing.

6. **Prepare for Integration Beyond the Org Chart**

- Understand that merging two firms, even small ones, requires real planning: tech stack, client service, compliance, and branding all need coordination.
- Have joint working sessions with operations and service teams before the transition is announced.
- Document new SOPs and internal workflows that reflect the combined firm's reality.

7. **Anticipate Personality Differences and Create Guardrails**

- Personality mismatches often derail peer-to-peer transitions.
- Use personality tools (DISC, Kolbe, Enneagram, etc.) to explore differences in leadership, communication, and problem-solving styles.
- Establish a conflict resolution process or advisory board to help mediate if friction arises.

8. **Communicate the Merger to Clients with Clarity and Confidence**

- Share the *story*: why this person, what it means for them, and how continuity is protected.

- Use co-branded materials, joint client meetings, and targeted messaging based on relationship depth.
- Make it easy for clients to feel reassured and stay engaged.

Option 2: Sell to an Aggregator

Aggregators focus on acquiring other firms while allowing the selling firm to retain their brand, culture, and leadership. Aggregators are typically "hands-off" when it comes to daily operations. They provide capital, resources, and infrastructure while letting you run your business with relative autonomy.

Think of it as joining a platform, not merging into a firm (even though you are).

Pros of Selling to an Aggregator	Cons of Selling to an Aggregator
Retain your leadership role and your team structure	Still requires leadership and management energy from the founder
Keep your brand and local identity	Won't gain total access to shared services: compliance, HR, tech, operations
Access to a broader advisor network for peer support	Some aggregators lack a clear post-acquisition integration process
Ability to tap into strategic resources to accelerate growth	

There are a few best practices to keep in mind when transitioning to an Aggregator:

1. **Ask Clear Questions About Operational Independence Post-Sale**

   - Clarify which decisions stay with you and which shift to the aggregator.
   - Ask about hiring authority, compensation models, marketing freedom, and investment platform requirements.
   - Determine whether compliance, tech, or service tools are mandatory or optional.

2. **Understand Performance Expectations and Long-Term Strategy**

   - Ask about revenue growth targets, profitability expectations, or integration milestones tied to your deal.
   - Understand how the aggregator defines success and how often it's measured.
   - Learn whether the aggregator is PE-backed and what their exit timeline or monetization strategy looks like.

3. **Learn What an Exit Looks Like If It's Not the Right Fit**

   - Ask what happens if you want to exit the relationship or buy your firm back.
   - Review buyback clauses, non-competes, and any golden handcuff structures.

- Talk through how others have exited and what that process looked like.

4. **Talk to Other Firms That Have Been Acquired**

- Reach out to peers who have already sold to the aggregator.
- Ask about the onboarding experience, post-close autonomy, and cultural alignment.
- Find out if their expectations were met, exceeded, or missed.

5. **Define Your Role and Timeline Clearly in Advance**

- Clarify your post-sale responsibilities and how long you plan to remain active.
- Align expectations for leadership, internal succession, and your team's future role.
- Be realistic about how much operational energy you'll still need to provide.

6. **Prepare Your Team Before the Announcement**

- Even if the brand and leadership stay the same, cultural and operational shifts may follow.
- Build an internal communication plan to keep staff informed and engaged.

- Involve key team members early in the due diligence process to build buy-in and reduce fear.

Option 3: Sell to an Integrator

Integrators go well beyond the aggregator model. Integrators absorb your practice fully into their systems, culture, brand, and leadership. Your business becomes part of their firm. This option is ideal for advisors who want a complete exit or are ready to hand over control and let someone else lead.

Pros of Selling to an Integrator	Cons of Selling to an Integrator
Strong operational resources and back-end support	Loss of your firm's brand, leadership identity, and voice
Centralized, proven infrastructure and systems	Less flexibility in how clients are served or how your team operates
Immediate relief from management and leadership burden	Must align closely with integrator's culture, systems, and goals

There are a few best practices to keep in mind when transitioning to an Integrator:

1. **Ask What Will Change and What Will Stay the Same**

   - Clarify how your clients will be served after the transition.
   - Understand how your team will be managed, compensated, and positioned within the new structure.
   - Confirm which of your current systems and processes will be replaced, and which may be retained temporarily.

2. **Talk to Multiple Firms and Former Sellers Before Committing**

   - Compare integrators based on leadership philosophy, client service approach, and cultural fit.
   - Reach out to advisors who have sold into each firm to learn what the integration actually felt like.
   - Ask about transition support, communication, and whether expectations were met post-sale.

3. **Get Clarity on the Back-End Multiples for Your Full Payout**

   - Understand what milestones or performance targets are required to receive your full valuation.
   - Clarify how client retention, revenue, or team stability is tracked and measured.

- Ask how and when the remaining payout will be calculated, and what could reduce it.

4. **Protect Non-Negotiables in the Deal Structure**

- Define what aspects of your client service model must be preserved.
- Include cultural or philosophical non-negotiables in writing, not just verbal agreements.
- Consider exit clauses or earnout protections if expectations around culture or service are not upheld.

More on Aggregators vs. Integrators

Listen to "Decoding Aggregators, Integrators, and the PE Play" for more info on the tradeoffs, timelines, and expectations behind the deal.

Option 4: Sell to a Private Equity Firm

Private equity firms bring capital, structure, and a clear growth plan. They typically partner with or acquire practices as part of a larger investment strategy.

Pros of Selling to a Private Equity Firm	Cons of Selling to a Private Equity Firm
High Valuations	Earnout periods can create stress and misaligned incentives
Attractive cash offers	Your team may struggle to adjust to a performance-driven environment
Often less emotionally complicated than internal sales	Risk of multiple ownership changes within a short time frame
	May deprioritize original vision and client approach

There are a few best practices to keep in mind when transitioning to a Private Equity Firm:

1. **Know Your Walkaway Number**

- Define your minimum acceptable deal terms before engaging in serious discussions.
- Factor in taxes, payout structure, and post-sale involvement to arrive at a net figure.
- Avoid being swayed by inflated valuations that come with complex earnout risks.

2. **Have Legal and Valuation Experts on Your Side**

   - Hire an attorney experienced in PE-backed advisory firm deals.
   - Use a third-party valuation firm to validate assumptions and protect your upside.
   - Ensure all financial terms, contingencies, and earnout triggers are clearly defined in the agreement.

3. **Vet the PE Firm's Long-Term Vision and Reputation**

   - Understand whether they plan to flip the business, hold on to it long-term, or roll it into another deal.
   - Ask about their track record with past advisor acquisitions, especially team and client retention.
   - Look into the firm's leadership philosophy, cultural values, and growth strategy.

4. **Ask to Speak with Other Advisors They've Acquired**

   - Reach out to founders who have sold to this PE firm in the past 3–5 years.
   - Ask about the onboarding process, earnout experience, and cultural integration.
   - Get insight into how their role, team, and clients were treated after closing.

5. **Include Client and Team Experience in the Valuation Equation**

- Push for a deal structure that values continuity.
- Negotiate provisions that protect your team's roles, compensation, and advancement.
- Advocate for a client experience standard that preserves trust and legacy.

Option 5: Combine Options

Some advisors take a hybrid approach. They sell a portion of the business externally while elevating internal talent into leadership. Others bring in an external firm to acquire the business but retain key staff, systems, or branding.

Pros of Selling to a Private Equity Firm	Cons of Selling to a Private Equity Firm
Balanced control and support	Complex negotiation and role definitions
Preserves internal relationships while creating liquidity	Requires strong leadership on both sides
Flexibility in deal structure and role clarity	Can blur lines of authority or vision if not managed well

There are a few best practices to keep in mind when combining succession options:

1. **Create Clear Swim Lanes for Internal and External Leaders**

   - Define decision-making authority across operations, client service, and strategic direction.
   - Clarify roles between the internal team and external partner to avoid overlap or confusion.
   - Ensure leadership responsibilities are aligned with each person's strengths and capacity.

2. **Ensure Cultural Alignment and Shared Expectations**

   - Align on firm values, client service philosophy, and long-term vision before finalizing the deal.
   - Facilitate planning sessions with both internal and external stakeholders to build trust and clarity.
   - Use joint working sessions or retreats to unify leadership before rollout.

3. **Define Who Owns What and When That Changes**

- Document which ownership percentages that transfer immediately and that are tied to future milestones.
- Clarify vesting schedules, equity earn-ins, and exit opportunities for internal successors.
- Identify the point at which control shifts, and what governance model supports that.

4. **Communicate Openly with Your Team and Clients**

- Share the reasons behind the blended strategy to build confidence and reduce uncertainty.
- Be transparent about leadership roles, branding decisions, and how client service will be maintained.
- Reinforce how the structure supports continuity, opportunity, and long-term relationships.

External Doesn't Mean Impersonal

Choosing an external path doesn't mean you're giving up on your legacy. In fact, it might be the clearest way to protect it. Done right, an external transition can give your clients more resources, your team more opportunity, and you more peace of mind.

External Succession Comparison

Succession Option	Best Fit For	Pros	Cons
Sell to an Advisor/ Peer	Shared values, local integration	• Key fit • Flexible terms	• Readiness issues • Potential clashes
Sell to an Aggregator	Autonomy with back-end support	• Keep your brand • Access to capital	• Less integration support
Sell to an Integrator	Complete exit or full absorption	• Turnkey opportunities • Relief from Leadership	• Loss of brand • Loss of flexibility
Sell to Private Equity Firm	Max cash-out with strategic partner	• High valuations • Liquidity	• Earnouts • Cultural misalignments
Combine Options	Hybrid between internal and external	• Flexibility • Balanced control	• Complexity in governance • Complexity in roles

Don't let guilt or old narratives hold you back. You're not abandoning your firm. You're ensuring it continues to thrive even when you're no longer at the center. You have options. Now it's time to choose the one that serves your future best.

CONCLUSION

Which Path Will You Choose?

You started this book with one certainty: You *will* exit. What you may not have known then (or been ready to admit) is how many options you have, and how much power you still hold in shaping what comes next. Maybe you picked up this book because you felt the pressure building. Your team started asking questions. Your clients sensed a change. Your spouse wondered what the future looks like. Or maybe you were just feeling that subtle but persistent knowing: *It's time to start thinking about what comes after this.*

Whether you're a decade away from retiring or thinking about stepping back next year, the decision you make today matters. In fact, the earlier you engage in the process, the more freedom, leverage, and peace of mind you'll have.

For too long, succession has been treated like a one-size-fits-all checklist: pick a successor, sign the docs, and ride into the sunset. But if you've spent decades building a practice, shaping a culture, and walking alongside clients through the most important moments of their lives, you know it's not that simple.

Succession is more of a transformation and less of a checklist.

It doesn't happen in one conversation, one quarter, or even one year. It unfolds slowly through mindset shifts, strategy changes, and courageous conversations, through internal work first, and then decisions.

You don't have to drift. You don't have to default to what everyone else does. You don't have to delay because you're afraid of letting people down. And you definitely don't have to wait until something forces your hand.

You can lead your own exit, and you can do it in a way that honors your clients, rewards your career, protects your team and family, and opens up a new life that's built on purpose. You can build a succession plan that gives you the freedom you deserve without sacrificing what you spent a lifetime creating. You can model the very thing you've helped clients do all these years: exit with clarity, confidence, and grace.

There is no perfect path, but there is a right path for *you.*

What matters most is that you choose it intentionally, courageously, and with the same clarity you've offered to so many others over the years.

So now, the only question left is the one you saw at the very beginning:

Will you lead your exit, or will your exit lead you?

Take what you've seen here, gather your family and team, and have the conversations. Ask the questions you've been avoiding, and then choose. The next chapter of your life is already being written. Make sure it's the one you want.

ADDITIONAL SUCCESSION PLANNING RESOURCES

As you move into this section, I want to be transparent about something: The list below contains the same resources I used (and still use) in my own succession planning. Nothing I've shared was theoretical for me. I needed tools and an outside perspective to help me stay accountable, see blind spots, and keep moving forward. The resources you're about to review are the ones that made the biggest difference in my journey.

Look for tools and resources at totalsuccession.com:

- Listen to the Total Succession podcast
- Sign up for the Total Succession newsletter
- Get information about succession coaching
- Find more information on the resources below:

Coaching

I've worked with several coaching organizations over the years. Each played a different role: some helped me grow as a leader, others helped me think more strategically about the business, and some pushed me to get out of my own way. Coaching gave me accountability, clarity, and momentum during the parts of succession that felt overwhelming.

- Strategic Coach - strategiccoach.com
- Ironstone Business Coaching - ironstonehq.com
- Pareto Systems - paretosystem.com
- ClientWise - clientwise.com
- Your Legacy Partners - yourlegacypartners.com
- Truest Fan Coaching - truestfan.com

Vision Casting

Before I could prepare the business, I had to understand what I wanted next. A few questions helped me slow down long enough to define a vision for my life after the firm. Without that clarity, I wouldn't have been able to make good decisions or communicate them well.

I've put those questions on the SPACE Starter Worksheet. It's a free, simple tool I created to help you begin naming what you want to preserve, and what you're ready to release. Download the worksheet here:

Succession Planning Worksheet
Walk through the "See" and "Prepare" phases of the SPACE framework to define your vision and assess your readiness. Scan the code to view or download.

G2 Hiring & Development

The next-generation team at FORM Wealth Advisors didn't happen by accident. We built a career path, an internship program, and a mentorship model that allows younger advisors to grow with us. This continues to develop as our team grows, but these resources reflect exactly how we developed our own G2 bench and why it mattered.

How to Build Your Bench

Learn how to build next-gen talent from the ground up in this episode: A 5-Stage Path to Building Advisor Talent from Within.

POPULAR

Practice Valuation & Financing

The need for real valuation was one of the biggest wake-up calls in my own planning. I needed more than a guess. These firms provided objective guidance on financing options. They helped me think through deal structure, timing, taxes, and how to make the transition fair for everyone involved.

- Wise Rhino Group - wiserhinogroup.com
- Spruce Rock Capital - sprucerockcapital.com

EOS Implementation

EOS brought structure, accountability, and clarity to our operations with delegation, documentation, and people systems. It helped us build a business that could run without me. An essential step for creating a transferable, succession-ready firm.

- EOS Implementor: Andrea Schlapia of Ironstone Business Coaching

Structure Builds Trust

Hear Andrea Schlapia talk about how tools like EOS help founders get out of their own way and build succession-ready firms. Scan to listen!

I'm giving you these resources for one reason: I don't want you to build your succession plan in isolation. These tools and partners helped me make better decisions, stay consistent, and keep my clients protected while my firm transitioned into its next chapter.

My hope is that they'll give you the same clarity and confidence as you create your own path forward.

APPENDIX

Succession Path	Best Fit For	Pros	Cons
Sell to a Team Member	Strong internal talent ready for ownership	• Client continuity • Cultural alignment • Gradual transition	• Financing Limitations • Entitlement risk • Long deal timelines
Sell to a Family Member	Family in the business with interest in succession	• Preserves Legacy • Shared values • High emotion meaning	• Resentment risk • Potential misalignment • Family/business tension
Sell to Another Team on Same BD/ Platform	Advisors looking for scale with internal familiarity	• Shared systems • Flexible ownership • Partial exit possibility	• Role confusion • Turf tension • Cultural blend required
Sell to Peer or Local Advisor	Known peer or trusted colleague in region or network	• Cultural fit • Flexible deal terms • Shared model familiarity	• Readiness unclear • Leadership/style clashes • Integration risk
Sell to an Aggregator	Want capital resources but keep autonomy	• Keep your brand • Access to capital • Peer Network	• Post-sale work still required • Limited integration support
Sell to an Integrator	Ready to fully exit and hand over leadership	• Strong systems • No leadership burden • Scalable infrastructure	• Loss of brand/voice • Requires cultural alignment
Sell to Private Equity Firm	Seeking high valuation and cash liquidity	• High payout • Strategic growth support	• Earnout stress • Performance-driven culture • Potential ownership shifts
Combine Internal and External	Want to elevate team while bringing in outside capital	• Balanced control • Retain talent • Flexible Structure	• Complex governance • Dual Leadership challenges

ENDNOTES

1   Henricks, Mark. *Smart Asset.* "Financial Advisor
    Industry Statistics to Know." March 3, 2025.
    https://smartasset.com/advisor-resources/
    how-many-financial-advisors-in-the-us.

2   McKinsey & Company. *McKinsey & Company.*
    "The Looming Financial Advisor Shortage
    in US Wealth Management." February
    10, 2025. https://www.mckinsey.com/
    industries/financial-services/our-insights/
    the-looming-advisor-shortage-in-us-
    wealth-management

3   The Cartograph Group, Canaccord Genuity
    Wealth Management. *CG Wealth Management.*
    "Why Your Wealth Advisor's Succession Plan
    Is Crucial for Your Family's Financial Future"
    October 10, 2025. https://thecartographgroup.
    com/why-your-wealth-advisors-succession-plan-
    is-crucial-for-your-familys-financial-future/

4   Donovan, Paul. *World Economic Forum.*
    "What does the Great Wealth Transfer Mean
    for Economic Growth?" September 30, 2025.
    https://www.weforum.org/stories/2025/09/
    great-wealth-transfer-economic-growth/.

ACKNOWLEDGMENTS

This book would not exist without the conversations, generosity, and wisdom of the people listed below. Each of you shaped this journey with your insights, your candor, and your commitment to helping advisors navigate succession with clarity and courage. I'm deeply grateful for your time, trust, and belief in my mission.

Scott W. Danner
Steward Partners

Aaron Hasler
Spruce Rock Capital

David Patchen
GBED Enterprises LLC

Ted Motheral
Formerly of The Potomac Law Group

Andrea Schlapia
Ironstone Business Coaching

Rob Brown
Truest Fan Coaching

Peter Campagna
Wise Rhino Group

Duncan MacPherson
Pareto Systems

Ray Sclafani
ClientWise

Bryan Sweet
Sweet Financial Partners

Nick Arellano
Your Legacy Partners

Dean Smith
Wealth Enhancement

Brittany Anderson
Sweet Financial Partners

Nate Lenz
Concurrent

Alex Goss
NewEdge Advisors

Brian Church
OneAscent & Advisory DNA

Start Here!

DOWNLOAD THIS WORKSHEET

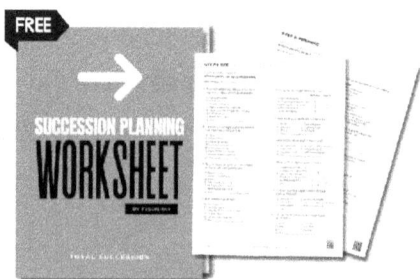

This worksheet will help you take the first and most important step in exit planning: *getting clear on what you want*.

You'll walk through the "See" and "Prepare" phases of the SPACE framework to define your vision and assess your readiness.

Scan the code to view and download ↓

totalsuccession.com/worksheet

Get Real Succession Strategies. Anytime, Anywhere.

Short, practical episodes designed for busy advisors planning their future.

TOTAL SUCCESSION
WITH TYSON RAY

WATCH ON ▶ YouTube

Listen on
Apple Podcasts

LISTEN ON Spotify

TOTALSUCCESSION.COM/PODCAST

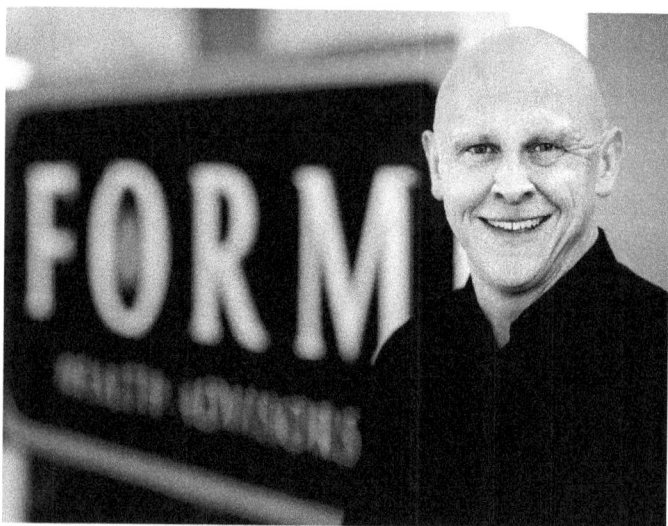

Succession isn't optional.

You *will* exit your practice. Will you lead it, or will it lead you? Follow Tyson Ray on LinkedIn for proven strategies from an advisor who's been there.

Scan the code to view Tyson's profile ↓

linkedin.com/in/tysonray

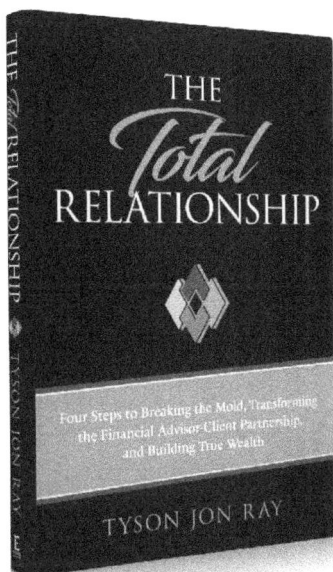

THE *Total* RELATIONSHIP

Four Steps to Breaking the Mold, Transforming the Financial Advisor-Client Partnership, and Building True Wealth

TYSON JON RAY

www.ingramcontent.com/pod-product-compliance
Lightning Source LLC
Chambersburg PA
CBHW071430210326
41597CB00020B/3729